# Clean Eating Diet

## Your One-Stop Clean Eating Cookbook with Clean Eating Recipes for Every Meal

Linda Williams

# Table of Contents

## CHAPTER 6: CLEAN EATING RECIPES FOR BREAKFAST ................................................................. 63

## CHAPTER 7: CLEAN EATING DIET RECIPES FOR APPETIZERS AND SNACKS ........................................... 76

## CHAPTER 8: DELECTABLE DESSERT CLEAN EATING RECIPES ................................................................... 93

## CHAPTER 9: EASY CLEAN DIET 5-DAY MEAL PLAN.. 103

NV

# Introduction

Although many Americans find themselves dieting on a regular basis, most people never end up losing the fat and weight they really want to. Even though most people continue to diet on a regular basis, obesity, diabetes, metabolic syndrome and heart disease are all prevalent. Clean eating offers a simple way to approach nutrition and dieting that really works. It is a healthy diet plan that emphasizes eating nutritious, sensible meals. It provides a tasty, easy way to begin getting healthier.

Of course, when embarking on the clean eating diet, you may not be sure how the diet works, what you can eat or how to begin clean cooking. This clean eating cookbook is packed with helpful information on the clean eating diet, benefits of this diet, helpful cooking tips and plenty of great recipes that you can use for any meal. From main dishes to delectable desserts, you will find many clean eating recipes that you can use to help you ensure you stick to your clean eating diet plant.

# Chapter 1: What is the Clean Eating Diet?

Believe it or not, the clean eating diet is not a new diet plan. It has been used for many years, although it has recently become more popular. Many people credit Tosca Reno, a Canadian author and fitness model, with making this approach popular. However, this diet has actually been along for decades.

So, what exactly is clean eating? How does it work? It is actually pretty simple. First, the diet focuses on eating foods that are unrefined, unprocessed and whole. This means that the foods are as close as possible to the form the foods appear in out in nature. The diet also focuses on avoiding processed sugars, especially sodas. On the diet, you will focus in eating healthy fats and avoiding the unhealthy trans fats and saturated fats.

The clean eating diet also includes combining lean protein and complex carbohydrates together at each meal. It also stresses eating to get as many nutrients as possible while avoiding foods that are essentially "empty" calories, such as cookies, processed snacks, sodas and fast foods. You also need to learn to pay attention to the right portion sizes while ensuring you practice good portion control. This diet also requires you to drink plenty of water to keep your body well hydrated. The basics of this diet are very simple and easy to remember as you embark on this new way of eating.

## The Pros and Cons of the Diet

When you are considering a new diet, it is always a good idea to look at the pros and cons that the diet offers. The good news is that the clean eating diet comes with many great pros and few cons. Of course, it is still important to consider both sides so you can decide if this diet will work well for you and your family.

### The Pros

- You eat frequent smaller meals through your day, which helps to keep you from getting too hungry. You get high quality nutrition on a regular basis.

- Another pro is that the diet focuses on a very balanced diet. You will be getting a balanced intake of foods from each food group.

- It is easy to find great clean eating recipes and menu planning resources that help you to follow the diet.

- The diet focuses on eating unprocessed foods and notes that eating this way helps you feel better, improves your overall health and also helps to improve appearance.

- You will begin learning more about the right portion sizes, making it easier for you to know how much you should be eating.

- The clean eating diet also emphasizes how important it is for you to consume enough essential fatty acids on a regular basis.

**The Cons**

- The clean eating diet plan is actually pretty stringent, even though it can be easy to follow. You will need to give up processed foods, including sugars, alcohol, prepared foods and refined carbs.

- When on the diet, it can interfere with you eating out with others. It can be difficult to find restaurants that serve meals that will go along with the clean eating plan. However, that is not really a good reason to avoid the plan.

# Chapter 2: Benefits of Clean Eating

If you decide to go on the clean eating diet, you may want to know more about the benefits this diet has to offer. While it may seem pretty stringent at first, it offers so many great benefits. The following are just a few of the proven benefits that you can enjoy when you embark on a clean eating journey. Plus, the following recipes within this clean eating cookbook make it easy to follow the diet plan without giving up flavorful, delicious foods.

Benefit #1 – Increase Muscle – Since the diet focuses on eating plenty of protein with each meal, you will be able to increase muscle. Protein is important for muscle building, so this diet can help you to increase your overall lean muscle tissue.

Benefit #2 – Reduce Body Fat – Another of the benefits of clean eating is the ability to decrease body fat. Since you cut out unhealthy fats, it makes it much easier to lose fat. It also cuts out processed sugars, which are often stored as fat. Cutting out all that sugar can help you to eliminate fat, helping you to lose weight. The great focus on portion sizes also helps individuals to reduce overall body fat, losing weight and feeling better about themselves.

Benefit #3 – Overall Improved Health – The clean eating diet is all about getting the most nutrition from your diet. When you focus on eating foods that contain important nutrients and vitamins, you can easily improve the overall health of your body.

Benefit #4 – Reduced Risk of Diseases – When you go on this clean eating plan, you will also enjoy the benefit of a reduced risk of various diseases. Avoiding unhealthy foods will help you to reduce your risk of certain cancers, diabetes, heart disease, obesity and stroke.

Benefit #5 – Easy to Sustain – Many fad diets can be difficult to continue following after some time. However, the clean eating diet is actually sustainable. Since it follows a holistic approach to eating, it makes the diet easy to follow for your entire life. You do not just go on this diet. This is a diet that can become an entire lifestyle that improves your life in many ways.

Benefit #6 – Increased Energy – Most people that go on the clean eating diet report that they enjoy increased energy within a few days. You may be surprised to find out how all those processed, sugary foods were sapping your energy. When you start eating clean and you begin eating wholesome foods that are packed with important vitamins and nutrients, your energy levels will soar and make you feel much better. This makes it easier for you to get active, since you will have the energy needed to exercise on a regular basis.

# Chapter 3: Clean Eating Diet Tips

Going on the clean eating diet can take some work on your part. It is not easy to simply change the way you eat. If you are just starting out, these clean eating diet tips can be a huge help. You'll find helpful planning tips, preparation, food lists and other essential tips to help you successfully make the change to clean eating.

**Planning is Essential**

If you are going to succeed on the clean eating diet, it is so important to begin planning ahead of time. With some careful planning, you can ensure you are successful as you make the transition. The following are a few helpful planning tips:

- Plan ahead to eat 4-6 meals every day. This will take some planning, since you'll need to add in some extra small meals.

- Start by cleaning out your pantry ahead of time. Get rid of any high sugar foods, refined foods, high fat foods and processed foods so you will not be tempted to begin eating them again.

- When you are ready to go shopping for clean eating ingredients, make sure that you plan a shopping list and plan a menu for the week. This way you know what you need to buy and you have the ingredients on hand to make clean eating recipes.

- Once you are at the grocery store, work your way around the perimeter of the store where you will find clean, wholesome ingredients. Processed foods are found in the center of the store, so avoid that area so you do not get tempted to buy those foods.

**Preparing**

Preparing for your meals can definitely help you become more successful when you begin clean eating. Here are some essential preparation tips:

- Avoid going hungry if you do not have clean eating foods available. Make sure you have an apple or some almonds with you at all times so you do not get hungry and binge on something you should not be eating.

- Work to prepare meals in advance. Before you go to bed, prepare your lunch for the next day so you do not get up with little time and choose something that goes against your clean eating diet. It is also nice to prepare for dinners in advance by prepping ingredients ahead of time or preparing full meals you can simply pop in the oven.

- Eat every 2-4 hours to keep yourself feeling full. This will help to prevent binging.

Other Important Tips for Success

- Focus on portion sizes. One of the main parts of the clean eating diet is learning proper portion control. Since restaurants serve such huge portions today, it is easy to be unaware of what proper portion sizes actually are. Educate yourself on proper portion sizes, which will help you be more successful with this diet.

- Know your own hunger cues. Everyone has their own hunger cues but most people happen to ignore them. Many people eat when they are not hungry and keep eating when their hunger has actually been sated. Part of eating the clean diet is to make sure you eat when you feel hungry and avoiding overeating. Think about your hunger cues before you begin eating and pay attention to your body so you really know when you are full.

- Learn to use spices and herbs in your cooking. Look for clean eating recipes that use herbs and spices. When you are used to eating processed foods, you get used to all the fat and the unnatural flavors. When you begin clean eating, you want to avoid using flavorings that are unhealthy. You can make clean ingredients taste amazing by using herbs and spices in your recipe. Spices and herbs can be used as rubs, to flavor vegetables and more.

**Your Helpful Clean Foods List**

If you are not sure what foods are part of the clean eating diet, here is a list of a few of the main clean eating foods you are allowed to eat on the diet. Of course, this list does not cover every food, but it will give you a great start.

Clean Eating Proteins

- Fish
- Chicken
- Top round beef
- Tofu
- Eggs
- Turkey
- Shellfish

Clean Eating Carbs

- Brown rice
- Whole wheat pasta
- Rice pasta
- Quinoa
- Whole Wheat (100%)
- Oatmeal
- Corn Torillas
- Sprouted Grains
- Coconut, Almond, Rice, Spelt or Oat Flour

## Clean Eating Diary

- Greek Yogurt
- Cottage Cheese
- Almond Milk

## Clean Eating Veggies and Fruits

- Lentils
- Apples
- Dried Fruits
- Leafy Greens
- All Veggies
- Avocados
- Bananas
- Oranges
- Berries
- All other fruits

## Clean Eating Nuts

- Cashews
- Peanuts
- Seeds
- Almonds
- Walnuts
- Almond and Peanut butter (all natural)

## Clean Eating Oils

- Sunflower Oil
- Olive Oil
- Coconut Oil

## Clean Eating Sweeteners

- Pure maple syrup
- Raw Stevia
- Honey

# Chapter 4: Tasty Main Dish Clean Eating Recipes

## Clean Eating Baked Bowtie Pasta Recipe

With whole wheat pasta, this meal will fit in with your clean eating diet pan. You can change up the protein in the recipe for your favorite flavor. This recipe works best with your diet if you make your own homemade pasta sauce from fresh, clean eating approved ingredients. It is a full meal, but it is nice to add a nice vegetable salad on the side to add even more veggies to the meal.

**What You'll Need:**

    1 lb. of ground beef, lean (or venison)
    1 pound of whole wheat bowties
    32 oz. of tomato sauce (your choice)
    1 cup of mozzarella cheese, freshly grated
    ½ cup of onion, chopped
    ½ cup of Parmesan cheese, grated
    Nonstick cooking spray

**How to Make It:**

Preheat your oven to 350F.

Cook meat in a skillet until well browned, draining any grease from the meat. Add the onion and tomato sauce to the meat, allowing to simmer slowly for about 10 minutes. Cook pasta according to package directions. Once pasta is cooked and drained, add it to the sauce and meat, blending together well.

Prepare a 9x13 baking dish with cooking spray. Spread half of the pasta and sauce mix into the pan, sprinkling with half of the grated Parmesan. Add the rest of the past, topping with the rest of the Parmesan. Cover the dish with foil, baking at 350 for about 15 minutes. The cheese should be totally melted and slightly browned.

## Clean Eating Grilled Chicken Burrito

This recipe is a great lunch idea, but it is heavy enough to make a nice dinner as well. Full of great veggies, it proves to be a wonderful way to get kids to eat more vegetables. Experiment with different burrito toppings for a variety of different flavors with this recipe.

**What You'll Need:**

6 oz. of chicken breast, boneless and skinless
1/2 cup of chopped tomatoes
2 tbsp. of chopped cilantro
2 tbsp. of chopped red onion
1/2 cup of shredded iceburg lettuce
1 whole wheat tortilla
1/8 an avocado

**How to Make It:**

Preheat the oven to 350 degrees F. Bake in the oven for 20 minutes. Allow the chicken breast to cool, then slicing into very thin slices. Take the tortilla, covering with paper towels, then microwaving for about 8-10 seconds or until soft and warm. Place all ingredients into the tortilla, wrap up and then enjoy.

# Easy Clean Eating Flank Steak Recipe (gluten free too)

Flank steak makes a great addition to your clean eating recipe book because it is such a great lean cut of meat. It also packs in plenty of protein, with every serving providing 33 grams of protein. This recipe adds plenty of flavor to the meat, which is goo with many different vegetable side dishes.

**What You'll Need:**

2 limes – juiced
2 seeded and diced red chile peppers
1 Tbsp. of extra virgin olive oil
Sea salt to taste
2 thinly sliced green onions
Freshly ground black pepper to taste
1 flank steak, approximately 32 ounces

**How to Make It:**

In a ziplock bag, add salt, pepper, olive oil, peppers, onions and lime juice. Next, place the flank steak into the bag as well, shaking and massaging to get the marinade into the flank steak. Place in the refrigerator, allowing to marinate for 2-3 hours.

Preheat a grill on high, gently oiling the grill grate. Remove steak from marinade, throwing away the marinade. Grill the steak over medium high heat for about 12-15 minutes. Flip about halfway through cooking. Once steak has finished cooking, place on a cutting board and allow it to rest for 5-7 minutes. Slice across the grain very thinly, serving up while warm. Makes approximately six servings.

# Red Onion Tenderloin Steaks Recipe

Tenderloin steaks turn out tender and delicious with this easy to make recipe. Serve up with green beans and mashed potatoes for a wonderful clean eating meal.

**What You'll Need:**

2 tablespoons of red wine vinegar
2 tablespoons of honey
1 teaspoon of dried thyme
1/4 teaspoon of freshly ground black pepper
½ teaspoon of salt, divided
1 large red onion, sliced thinly and then separated into rings
4 beef tenderloin steaks (4oz each)
Cooking spray

**How to Make It:**

Preheat the broiler.

In a large skillet, spray cooking spray and heat. Place onion in skillet, covering and allowing to cook for 3-4 minutes. Add honey, ¼ teaspoon of salt and vinegar to the onions. Allow to simmer on low for 8-10 minutes uncovered, stirring from time to time.

On beef tenderloins, sprinkle thyme, pepper and remaining salt. Place tenderloins on a broiler pan that has been prepared with cooking spray. Broil stakes for four minutes per side. Remove from oven when they reach desired doneness, serving hot with the prepared onion marmalade. Makes four servings.

# Fruity Salmon Recipe

This recipe is so easy to make but it tastes amazing and looks incredible on a plate. Quickly serve it up for clean dinner that comes together fast, making it perfect for a busy weeknight.

**What You'll Need:**

1 15 oz can of tropical fruit mix (DelMonte Tropical Fruit in 100% Juice is a great option)
Juice of 1/2 lemon
1 tablespoon olive oil
1 teaspoon fresh grated ginger (about a single 1 inch slice)
1 to 2 cloves garlic, minced
salt and pepper to taste
4 wild caught salmon fillets

**How to Make It:**

Preheat the oven to 350F.

In a shallow baking dish, place the salmon fillets. Top the salmon with lemon juice, garlic, tropical fruit, olive oil and the grated ginger. Sprinkle with a bit of salt and pepper to taste. Bake salmon for approximately 30 minutes or until the fish becomes flaky and tender. Serve while hot with a nice salad on the side. Makes four servings.

# Stir Fried Beef Recipe

For those that enjoy stir fries, this recipe is a delicious option to try. The recipe is easy and fast to make, offering a tasty meal that includes protein, veggies and a healthy form of carbs as well. Makes a great one pan meal.

## What You'll Need:

1 cup of yellow onion, chopped
3 cloves of garlic, minced
1 yellow pepper, chopped
1 green bell pepper, chopped
1 orange bell pepper, chopped
1 lb. of lean beef tenderloin, carefully trimmed and then sliced thinly
1 cup of roasted red peppers, chopped
Sea salt
Freshly ground black pepper
1 cup of beef broth (preferably low sodium)
¼ cup of fresh basil, chopped
1 cup of quinoa
1 Tbsp. of extra virgin olive oil

## How to Make It:

Cook the quinoa according to the directions on the package, setting to the side when finished.

While quinoa is cooking, heat the olive oil in a skill on medium high heat. Place garlic and onion in the pan, cooking for 3 minutes or until the onions soften. Add in the roasted and bell peppers, cooking for two more minutes while stirring. Place beef in the pan, cooking for two more minutes. Broth should now be added to the mix, allowing it to simmer for about two minutes until the steak has thoroughly cooked. Remove pan from heat, adding salt, pepper and basil. Serve the beef stir fry over the quinoa. Makes four servings.

# Vegetable Salmon Kabobs Recipe

If you are looking for a healthy, fast meal, this clean recipe makes a perfect weeknight meal that the entire family is sure to enjoy. It adds plenty of great veggies. Of course, you can always adapt this recipe to include other veggies that your family enjoys for a bit of a twist.

**What You'll Need:**

1 zucchini, sliced up into 1/4 in pieces
8 oz. of whole white mushrooms
Black pepper to taste
2 Tbsp. of parsley, chopped
Juice of 1 lemon
Sea salt to taste
Extra virgin olive oil
2 cups of brown rice
1 lb. of wild salmon fillets, cubed
1 medium white onion, cut into 1/2 in squares

**How to Make It:**

Prepare wooden skewers by soaking them for 20 minutes in water before using. If using metal skewers, this is not a problem.

Prepare the brown rice according to the directions on the package, setting to the side when finished.

Turn the broiler on high and allow to preheat. While the broiler is preheating, thread the veggies and salmon chunks onto four different skewers, alternating pieces. Brush completed skewers with the olive oil, then adding the lemon juice. Sprinkle parsley, pepper and salt over the skewers.

Place skewers in oven, broiling for about three minutes 2-4 inches from the broiler heat source. Turn and then allow to broil for about three more minutes or until the veggies are tender and the fish is fully cooked. Serve hot, serving a skewer over about a ½ cup of hot rice. Makes about four servings.

# Stuffed Mediterranean Chicken Breast Recipe

With just five ingredients, this recipe could not be easier to make. Ingredients are easy to find and add plenty of delicious flavor to the dish. Serve this up for your family or make it into an elegant entrée when serving up guests. Serve with fresh cooked green beans on the side. Easily serves eight, so it is a great recipe if you are serving several people.

**What You'll Need:**

2 tablespoons kalamata olives, pitted and finely chopped
1 tablespoon of fresh basil, minced
1 large red bell pepper
8 (6-ounce) chicken breasts, boneless and skinless
1/4 cup (1 ounce) crumbled feta cheese

**How to Make It:**

Preheat the broiler.

Take bell pepper, cutting it in half lengthwise, eliminating the membranes and seeds. On a foil lined cookie sheet, place pepper halves with their skin up, flattening out a bit with your hand. Broil the peppers for about 15 minutes or until the tops have blackened. Put blackened peppers into a ziplock bag, sealing and allowing to stand for another 15 minutes. After it stands, peel and finely chop the peppers for the smoky, roasted pepper flavor you will need in the recipe.

Turn on grill, preheating to medium high heat. Combine together the basil, cheese, olives and bell pepper.

Take chicken breasts, cutting a slit horizontally through the thickest area of every chicken breast half, creating a small pocket. Stuff the pocket with about 2 tablespoons of the pepper mixture, using a toothpick to close the opening so the stuffing will not fall out while cooking. Sprinkle chicken breasts with salt and pepper to taste.

Coat grill rack with cooking spray, then adding the chicken to the grill. Cook chicken for six minutes per side or until the chicken is fully cooked. Remove chicken from the grill, covering with foil loosely and allowing to stand for about 10 minutes before serving. Makes eight servings.

# Chopped Chicken Salad Recipe

This delicious salad is filling and full of healthy ingredients. It can be made quickly, making it a perfect main dish choice for dinner or for a nice lunch. If you make it for dinner, make enough for leftovers that you can enjoy the next day for lunch.

## What You'll Need:

1 medium size poblano pepper, seeded and then
2 cups of frozen corn
1 large sweet potato, peeled and then cubed
1/2 lb. chicken breast, boneless skinless, chopped
1 tablespoon of olive oil
1 teaspoon of cumin
1 can of black beans (15oz), drained and well rinsed
½ cup of low fat buttermilk
½ cup of low fat sour cream.
1 bunch of green onions, sliced thinly (separate green and white parts of the onion)
½ teaspoon of chile powder
4 romaine hearts, cut in half and then chopped
½ cup of cheddar cheese (low fat), grated

## How to Make It:

Preheat the oven to 450F.

Toss the potato, poblano peppers and corn with the olive oil in a medium-size bowl. On a prepared 9x13 baking dish, spread the vegetable mixture and roast at 450F for about 30 minutes. Every 10 minutes, use a spatula to toss the mixture. Roast until potato becomes soft and poblano peppers and corn begin to look a bit charred.

While roasting the veggies, in a large skillet, cook chicken for about 10 minutes, until it is cooked through and browned. Once browned, add in a ¼ cup of water, using water to scrape up the browned bits from the pan's bottom. Stir in the beans and the cumin. Cover the skillet, turning heat on low to keep the mixture warm until serving time.

To make the dressing, combined buttermilk, white onion parts, chile powder and sour cream together. Cover the bowl and place in the refrigerator to keep cool.

Once the vegetables are done roasting, remove and allow them to cool.

One four dinner plates, divide up the chopped romaine

lettuce. Top lettuce with the vegetables and chicken mixtures, dividing among the four plates. Top with cheese and green onions, then adding the refrigerated dressing. Makes four salads.

# Delicious BBQ Pork (or lamb) Recipe

This pork is perfectly barbequed and is wonderful as a main course served up with vegetables. If you have leftovers, this meal can be turned into a delicious sandwich for lunch, allowing you to get more from the meal.

**What You'll Need:**

¼ cup natural barbecue sauce and 8 teaspoons of the sauce, divided
1 ¼ pounds of pork (or lamb) tenderloin, boneless and trimmed
Garlic powder
Extra virgin olive oil
Black pepper to taste
Sea salt to taste

**How to Make It:**

Take the pork tenderloin, slicing it in half. Each crosswise half should be then cut in half lengthwise, which should create eight strips of the pork. Season the pork garlic powder, pepper and salt. Prepare a glass baking dish, placing the pork strips into the dish. Spoon the ¼ cup of natural barbecue sauce over the pork, ensuring the pork is fully coated. Cover the dish and allow to refrigerate for a minimum of six hours.

Preheat the oven's broiler. Take a baking sheet, lining it with aluminum foil and then lightly oiling it with some olive oil. Place marinated pork chops onto the baking sheet, ensuring that the strips are not touching. Broil strips for 2-3 minutes, then flipping them over to allow them to broil on the other side for approximately 2-3 more minutes. Pork should be fully cooked. Serve up the pork while warm with the leftover barbecue sauce as a dip.

# Grilled Scallops and Shrimp with Herbs Recipe

If you are in the mood for seafood, this tasty clean eating recipe makes the perfect main dish. You can change up the recipe by adding your own herb marinade as well for a totally different flavor. Another idea is to add in some vegetable wedges between the scallops and shrimp to add more vegetables to the recipe.

**What You'll Need**:

1 pound of uncooked medium shrimp that have been peeled and de-veined
1 pound of sea scallops
2 tablespoons of all natural Grapeseed Oil (Wildtree is a good brand)
1/2 cup of dry white vermouth
2 teaspoons of Wildtree Herb Grilling Marinade

**How to Make It:**

In a medium bowl, mix together the grapeseed oil and the herb grilling marinade. Add the scallops and the shrimp, allowing them to marinate for about 10-15 minutes and no longer. Place the scallops and shrimp onto skewers (soak wooden ones first) and then grill on medium. Serve with some couscous or some brown rice with a nice side salad. Makes 4 servings.

# Salsa, Black Bean Mexican Style Pizza Recipe

Yes, you can even enjoy pizza on the clean eating diet. This recipe is fully of amazing goodness and it is filling and easy to make. The black beans offer plenty of protein and fiber and you can add even more vegetables if you prefer.

**What You'll Need:**

4 teaspoons of olive oil
4 corn tortillas – 6-inch.
1 jalapeno pepper, seeded and then chopped finely while wearing gloves
½ cup of chopped onion
1 cup of canned black beans, rinsed and well drained
1 clove of garlic, minced
2 tablespoons of chopped cilantro, fresh
1 cup of tomato, seeded and chopped

**How to Make It:**

Preheat the oven to 425F.

On an ungreased baking sheet, lay out the corn tortillas, brushing them on all sides with about a teaspoon of olive oil. Bake in the oven for about 2-3 minutes on each side until they are crispy and nicely browned.

Meanwhile, cook the chile pepper, garlic and onion in a skillet, using the leftover olive oil. Allow to cook on medium until the onion becomes tender. Next, stir tomato and black beans into the mix, cooking until they are thoroughly heated.

Once tortillas are done, spoon the black bean mixture onto the tortillas. Place them back into the oven, allowing them to bake for about 4-5 more minutes. Remove from oven, topping with chopped cilantro before serving. Makes four servings.

# Chapter 5: Clean Eating Recipes for Delicious Side Dishes

## Roasted Squash, Kale and Quinoa Salad Recipe

The quinoa in this salad makes it extra filling. For plenty of flavor, the herbs, spice and a nice vinaigrette make it a delicious mix. With wonderful butternut squash and baby kale, you will get plenty of healthy nutrients from this delicious side dish.

**What You'll Need:**

1 tablespoon of olive oil
1 butternut squash (should way about 1.5 pounds)
2 cups of quinoa, cooked and cooled
1 apple, large and chopped coarsely
2 cups of baby kale, fresh and chopped coarsely
½ tablespoon of sea salt, preferably fine
1/3 cup of toasted pecans or almonds, chopped coarsely
Fresh ground black pepper, to taste

**For the Dressing:**

1 tablespoon of sherry vinegar
2 tablespoons of orange juice, fresh
2 tablespoons of extra virgin olive oil
Fresh ground black pepper, to taste
Pinch of dried thyme
Salt, to taste

**How to Make It:**

Preheat the oven to 375F.

Take the butternut squash, peeling it and eliminating the seeds. Cut the squash up into chunks that are about 1 inch square. Toss the squash chunks with the olive oil, sprinkling lightly with pepper and salt. Spread chunks on a rimmed baking pan, like a cookie sheet. Bake at 375 for about 15 minutes, taking the squash out and stirring thoroughly. Place back in the oven, allowing to bake another 15 minutes, or until lightly brown and tender. If it is not done yet, allow to bake for another 5-10 minutes. Allow the squash to cool.

Combine together the ingredients for the salad. Combine the baby kale, almonds, quinoa, apple and roasted squash in a large bowl.

Next, make the dressing for the salad. Use a jar to

combine together the thyme, pepper, salt, sherry vinegar, olive oil and orange juice. Place the lid on the jar, shaking until well combined. Pour dressing on the salad, mixing together to ensure the dressing reaches every part of the salad. Add some pepper and salt to taste. Makes about six cups.

# Crispy Roasted New Potatoes with Garlic Recipe

These crispy potatoes will make a great side dish for any meal. Keeping the slices nice and thin will ensure you get the crispy result in the end. Make plenty of these potatoes because everyone will want to eat plenty of them.

**What You'll Need:**

½ teaspoon of dried thyme
1 tablespoon of olive oil
2 cloves of garlic
1.5 pounds of red potatoes, sliced into slice about ¼ inch thick
Sea salt or coarse salt to taste

**How to Make It:**

Preheat the oven to 475F.

Mince the two cloves of garlic, sprinkling lightly with salt.

Now, use the flat of a knife to press the garlic until you make it into a thick paste. This can also be done using a garlic press and then using the flat of a knife. Place garlic paste in a little bowl. Combine olive oil and thyme with the garlic paste until combined.

Prepare a large baking sheet. In a large bowl, toss potatoes and garlic paste mixture together. Then, spread out the potatoes on a single layer on the baking sheet. Bake at 475 for about 25 minutes, ensuring potatoes are well browned on the bottom.

# Mozzarella Smothered Mushrooms Recipe

Portobello mushrooms provide a meaty, rich taste that is a great side dish instead of potatoes. Serve on the side with some kind of beef to add something special to the meal.

**What You'll Need:**

½ cup of salsa, low sodium preferred
2 tablespoons of sesame seeds
2 tablespoons of green onions, finely chopped
½ cup of mozzarella cheese, low fat
2 Portobello mushroom caps, gills and stems should be removed

**How to Make It:**

Preheat the oven to 400F.

On a baking tray, place the Portobello caps upside down. Top the caps with the green onions, cheese and salsa. Finally, top with the sesame seeds. Place in the oven, baking for about 10-12 minutes at 400F. Cheese should be well melted. Remove from oven, eating while warm. Makes two servings.

## Clean Eating Cole Slaw Recipe

If you love cole slaw, you'll enjoy this healthy version that is packed with delicious, healthy goodness.

**What You'll Need:**

1 tablespoon of turbinado sugar, plus 1 ½ teaspoons
¼ cup of low fat mayonnaise
¼ cup of apple cider vinegar
¼ cup of blue cheese, crumbled
¼ cup of sour cream, low fat preferred
½ teaspoon of Dijon mustard
8 ounces of coleslaw mix, shredded (or make your own)
Fresh black pepper and salt to taste

**How to Make It:**

Mix together the salt, sugar and vinegar in a saucepan, bringing the mixture to a boil. Allow the sugar to dissolve. Once it is fully dissolved, place coleslaw in a large bowl, pouring the hot mixture over the slaw. Toss well until all the mixture is coated with the sugar mixture.

Use a colander to drain the coleslaw, then placing it back in the large bowl. Toss the coleslaw with sour cream, mayo, blue cheese and mustard. Season to taste with pepper and salt. Place in the refrigerator, allowing to chill for a minimum of one hour before eating. Makes approximately four servings.

# Lentil and Greens Vegetarian Soup Recipe

This soup is full of great veggies. It is a comforting meal on a cool evening, but it can be served up all year long. This clean eating recipe has plenty of beautiful color with the tomatoes, fresh mushrooms and the Swiss chard included in the recipe.

**What You'll Need:**

8 ounces of cremini mushrooms, sliced thinly
1 cup of dry brown lentils, well rinsed and then drained
1 onion, chopped
1 bunch of rainbow Swiss chard, fresh
6 cups of water
2 tablespoons of olive oil
1 clove of garlic, chopped finely
1 tablespoon of soy sauce of tamari
1 ½ teaspoons of sea salt, fine
1 tablespoon of fresh lemon juice
½ teaspoon of dried thyme
1 cup of tomato, chopped
Cayenne pepper, to taste

**How to Make It:**

Use a large pot, heating up the olive oil on medium. Place the onion in the pan, allowing to cook for about three minutes or until it softens. Stir from time to time. Add in the garlic and mushrooms, cooking for another five minutes while stirring regularly. Next, add salt, thyme, water, oregano, cayenne and lentils. Bring the mixture to a boil. Once it comes to a boil, reduce the heat, allowing it to simmer for about 30-40 minutes uncovered. Lentils should be tender after this time.

While soup is cooking, take the Swiss chard and remove the stems, eliminating and woody parts from the stems. Chop up the stems coarsely, setting to the side. When the lentils have cooked until they are tender, add the stems of the Swiss chard to the soup, allowing to simmer gently for about five minutes. Then, add the tomatoes and Swiss chard leaves to the mix, allowing to simmer for another five minutes or until the laves have become tender. Last, stir in the tamari (or soy sauce) and the lemon juice.

Makes 9 cups of soup.

Note: Instead of the Swiss chard, you can use fresh kale instead, but you should only use the leaves of the kale if you decide to use kale. Do no use the stems of the kale.

# Blacked Eye Peas and Greens Side Dish Recipe

Combining black eyed peas with healthy greens gives you plenty of veggies and great protein and fiber at the same time. The red onion and tomato really adds to this side dish. If you do not want to use the suggested dressing recipe, you can always dress it with your own preferred dressing.

**What You'll Need:**

2 cups of mixed greens
6 cups of spinach, rinsed
1 tablespoon of chopped cilantro
½ cup of sliced red onion
1 teaspoon of Dijon mustard
1 diced tomato
2 tablespoons of extra virgin olive oil
1 tablespoon of red wine vinegar
1 minced clove of garlic
1 15oz can of black eyed peas, well rinsed and then drained.

**How to Make It:**

Combine together the cilantro, oil, vinegar, tomato,

garlic, mustard and garlic in a large bowl. Combine the ingredients by gently tossing them together. Use salt and pepper to season the mixture to taste.

Before serving, place the mixed greens and spinach in a large bowl, combined well. Top the greens with the bean mixture, combining by tossing gently. Serve. Makes four servings.

*Dried black eyed peas can be used, but they must be soaked overnight before using them in this recipe.

# Honey Glazed Baby Carrots

The addition of honey adds a hint of sweetness to the carrots, bringing out their full flavor. Since they offer plenty of vitamin A, carrots are a great veggie to add to any meal. Serve up as a delicious side that goes with many main dish recipes.

## What You'll Need:

3 tablespoons of olive oil
½ teaspoon of ground pepper
1 pound of baby carrots, trimmed and cleaned
1 tablespoon of lemon juice
½ teaspoon of ground ginger
2 ½ tablespoons of honey

## How to Make It:

Place carrots in a large saucepan, adding water so carrots are completely covered. Place a lid on the saucepan, bringing the water to a boil. Allow carrots to simmer until firm tender, which will take about five minutes. Drain the carrots, setting off to the side.

Heat olive oil up in a large skillet, then stirring the honey into the oil. Cook on low, stirring all the time until the honey is dissolved. Add remaining ingredients, combining well while stirring. Then, place the carrots in the skillet, gently tossing them around in the skillet until they are well coated. Allow to cook for about two minutes while stirring, ensuring that carrots are thoroughly heated.

Serve while hot. Makes 4 servings.

# Goat Cheese Roasted Sweet Potatoes Recipe

Sweet potatoes are full of great vitamins and the goat cheese and caramelized onions add incredible flavor to this vegetable side dish. It is easy to make, but to save time you can always prepare the dish the day before, baking when you are ready to serve it.

**What You'll Need:**

4 pounds of sweet potatoes, peel and then cut them into chunks ½ inch thick
Zest from an orange
1 thinly sliced, large red onion
2 tablespoons of extra virgin olive oil
2 ounces of crumbled goat cheese
1 tablespoon of honey
½ teaspoon of salt and 1/8 teaspoon of sea salt (divided)
3 tablespoons of panko bread crumbs, whole wheat
2 teaspoons of fresh thyme (divided)
4 tablespoons of orange juice (divided)
Black pepper to taste

**How to Make It:**

First, the oven racks need to be moved, placing one rack

in the oven's lower third and the other in the oven's upper third. Then, preheat oven to 425F.

Use parchment to line two cookie sheets. Divide up potatoes, placing them on both sheets. Each baking sheet of potatoes needs to be tossed with pepper, ¼ teaspoon of sea salt and ½ tablespoon of olive oil. Spread the potatoes out so they are laid into a single layer on the sheet. Place baking sheets in the oven – one on the lower rack and one on the top rack. Allow potatoes to roast for about 10 minutes.

Meanwhile, whisk the honey, juice and orange juice together in a little bowl.

After 10 minutes, remove the sweet potatoes, gently drizzling them with the orange mixture. Toss the potatoes and then spread them back into a single layer on the sheets. Place back in the oven, trading positions on the racks, continuing to roast for another 8-10 minutes. Potatoes should be tender and lightly browned. Remove from oven, setting to the side.

In a large skillet, heat up the rest of the olive oil, 1 tablespoon, adding the onion and using the last 1/8 teaspoon of salt to season it with some pepper to taste. Allow to cook while stirring until the onion becomes caramelized. This takes about 15 minutes.

Turn the oven down to 375F. Combine the potatoes with 1 ½ teaspoons of thyme and the last of the orange juice, spreading in an 11x7 baking dish. Top with the panko crumbs, onions and cheese. Place in the oven, baking until the potatoes are thoroughly heated and the cheese has melted and browned, about 20-25 minutes. Allow the potatoes to cool for about 7-10 minutes. Top with the leftover thyme. Serve at room temperature or you can serve while still warm. Makes approximately ten servings.

# Easy Baked Sweet Potato Fries Recipe

If you find yourself craving greasy French fries, these baked sweet potato fries will fit right into your clean eating diet. Not only are the delicious, but they are full of great nutrients, such as vitamin C, beta carotene and fiber. Sweet potatoes are better for you than white potatoes as well, since they have a lower glycemic index. Kids are sure to love having these baked fries as a tasty side dish.

**What You'll Need:**

½ teaspoon of dried oregano
1 pound of sweet potatoes
1 teaspoon of sea salt
½ teaspoon of paprika
¼ teaspoon of black pepper
2 tablespoons of olive oil

**How to Make It:**

Preheat the oven to 425F.

Take a non-stick cookie sheet and place it into the oven to heat.

Take the sweet potatoes and peel them, cutting into sticks that are ¼ inch wide and three inches in length. Take the sweet potato sticks, tossing them with the paprika, sea salt, black pepper, oregano and oil.

Spread out the potato sticks in a single layer on the preheated baking sheet, allowing to bake at 425 for 15 minutes. After baking for 15 minutes, turn over the fries, baking for another 15 minutes or until the fries are lightly browned. Turn with care, since potatoes will be quite soft.

Serve while hot.

## Sweet Potatoes Mashed Recipe

Instead of mashed white potatoes, these mashed sweet potatoes are a healthier option that can be added to any meal. They are especially delicious served up for thanksgiving or Christmas instead of sugary sweet potato dishes.

**What You'll Need:**

4 medium-size sweet potatoes
½ teaspoon of cinnamon
½ cup of fresh orange juice
½ teaspoon of ginger, ground
1 tablespoon of brown sugar
1 tablespoon of orange zest.

**How to Make It:**

Take sweet potatoes, peeling them and then cubing into 1-inch cubes. Place cubes of sweet potato in a large pot, covering with enough water to fully cover the potatoes.

Place potatoes on high heat, allowing the water to come to a rolling bowl. Continue cooking at a controlled boil until the potatoes become tender and fully cooked.

Use a colander to drain the sweet potatoes. Then, in a large bowl, combine the sweet potatoes with the remaining ingredients. Use a mixer to mash the ingredients until you have smooth, mashed sweet potatoes.

# Spanish Green Beans and Almonds Recipe

This side dish is full of flavor, thanks to the garlic and red onions added to the beans. Chopped almonds add a nice crunch to the dish. You can easily make this side dish and even kids will find it a tasty side that goes with many different main dishes.

## What You'll Need:

2 cloves of garlic, preferably fresh
¼ cup of water
2 pounds of green beans, fresh, trimmed and washed
1 tablespoon of oregano, fresh
2 tablespoons of olive oil
½ cup of almonds, chopped and then toasted
1 red onion, small, diced
Pepper and salt to taste

## How to Make It:

Heat the olive oil up in a saucepan on medium. Add beans, onion and garlic to the oil. After a couple minutes, the onion and garlic should begin browning. When this occurs, add the water to the pan. Place the top on the saucepan, allowing the beans to steam until they are tender. Once they reach desired tenderness, remove them from the heat.

Use pepper and salt to season the beans to taste. Sprinkle with the fresh oregano. Place beans on a serving platter, then topping with the toasted almonds. Serve while warm.

# Delicious Refried Beans for Clean Eating Recipe

Although these beans take a bit of time to prepare, they are quite simple to make. Make them on the weekend and enjoy serving them up during the week. Make sure you carefully pay attention when cooking the beans to avoid overcooking or burning them. They make a great side dish for Mexican style main dishes.

**What You'll Need:**

8 cups of water
¼ cup of onion, diced finely
1 ¼ cup of dried pinto beans
2 garlic cloves, minced
½ teaspoon of salt
1 jalapeno pepper, seeded, finely chopped while wearing gloves
2 tablespoons of olive oil

**How to Make It:**

Rinse dry beans thoroughly with water, eliminating bad beans and dirt. Combine the beans in a large pot with four cups of water. Allow to boil, then turn heat down, simmering while covered for about two minutes. Keep covered, but remove from the heat, allowing to stand for an hour. Drain and rinse the beans.

Use the same pot previously used, combining the last four cups of water, salt and the beans. Again, boil the beans, allowing the heat to be reduced so beans can simmer. Allow to simmer for about three hours, making sure beans become tender. Drain off the liquid from the beans, reserving the liquid.

Heat up the olive oil in a large skillet, adding the jalapeno, onion and garlic. Next, add the beans. Mash ingredients with a potato masher. Stir in about 1/3 cup of the reserved drained liquid, creating a paste. Continue to cook on low for about 10 minutes or until it reaches the thickness you prefer. Stir regularly to prevent burning.

Top with sour cream or cheddar cheese and serve on the side of a nice main dish. You can also use these beans in a dip or add to tacos for a delicious meal. Makes four ½ cup servings.

# Chapter 6: Clean Eating Recipes for Breakfast

## Oatmeal and Apple Pancakes Recipe

Pancakes are a wonderful way to start the day. The oatmeal adds more fiber to the pancakes, making them very filling. For some variation, you can substitute in other fruits instead of the apples for a different flavor that makes breakfast special.

**What You'll Need:**

1 ½ cup of whole wheat flour
2 tablespoons of baking powder
2 cups of water
3 apples, small
½ cup of oatmeal
1 teaspoon of nutmeg
1 teaspoon of vanilla or use to taste
1 teaspoon of cinnamon
¼ cup of chopped walnuts or pecans (optional)

**How to Make It:**

Peel the apples, then chopping them up fairly small. Put the apples in a pan, cooking them for a few minutes until they are soft. Use a potato masher to mash up the apples, allowing it to remain a bit chunky.

Mix together the dry ingredients in a medium bowl. Add the mashed apples and water to the bowl, stirring until all ingredients are well combined.

In a lightly greased, heated skillet, drop ¼ cup of the apple mixture. Cook until done on both sides. Makes approximately 10 pancakes, but may make less if you make pancakes larger.

# Mushroom and Sausage Mini Quiches Recipe

These mini quiches make a delicious, filling breakfast that is full of protein. They are wonderful for a nice brunch or even make great appetizers if you are having a party. Make extra quiches and freeze them individually. Then you can pop them out of the freezer to enjoy for a quick breakfast anytime.

**What You'll Need:**

8 ounces of white mushrooms, sliced
5 eggs and 3 egg whites
¼ cup of scallions, sliced
1 teaspoon of black pepper, freshly ground
1 cup of 1% or skim milk
1 teaspoon of extra virgin olive oil
¼ cup of Swiss cheese, shredded
8 ounces of chicken or turkey breakfast sausage, well chopped

**How to Make It:**

Preheat the oven to 325F.

Place the oven rack in the oven's center. Then, prepare a

12-cup muffin pan with cooking spray or you can use baking cups in the muffin pan.

In a large skillet that has been heated on medium high, place the sausage, allowing to cook until browned, which takes about 6-8 minutes. Place sausage in a bowl, allowing it to cool. Meanwhile, add the olive oil to the pan, placing mushrooms in the pan and cooking until browned. Add mushrooms to the bowl along with the sausage, allowing mushrooms to cool. Then, stir in the pepper, scallions and cheese.

In a medium-size bowl, whisk together the milk, egg whites and eggs. Fill muffin cups with the egg mixture. Top the egg mixture with some of the sausage mixture in every muffin cup.

Bake in the oven at 325 for 25 minutes, or until the tops of the muffins start to brown. Remove from oven, placing on a wire rack and allowing to cool for 4-5 minutes. Flip out the quiches carefully, allowing to cool completely. Then serve when cook. Makes a dozen quiches.

# Clean Eating Cranberry Lemon Muffins Recipe

This recipe makes a dozen muffins, allowing you to make them one day to enjoy for several days. The cranberry and lemon flavors combine together delightfully for a muffin that will make your taste buds sing in the morning.

**What You'll Need:**

¾ cup of plain yogurt, nonfat
3 teaspoons of lemon zest, fresh grated and divided
½ cup of sucanat sugar plust 2 tablespoons, divided
½ cup of cornmeal, fine or medium stone ground
1/3 cup of coconut oil
¼ teaspoon of sea salt
2 tablespoons of lemon juice, freshly squeezed
1 large egg
1 ½ cups of cranberries, frozen or fresh, chopped coarsely
1 ½ cups of whole-wheat, white flour
1 teaspoon of baking soda
2 teaspoons of baking powder

**How to Make It:**

Preheat the oven to 400F.

Use cooking spray to prepare a muffin tin or use paper liners.

In a medium-size bowl, whisk together egg, lemon juice, 2 tsp lemon zest, yogurt, oil and ½ cup of the sugar.

In a larger bowl, whisk the baking powder, salt, baking soda, cornmeal and flour together. Combine the yogurt mixture to the dry ingredients, folding together until nearly blended. Next, add the cranberries, folding into the batter. Place batter in the muffin cups, dividing up evenly.

In a small bowl, combine the last teaspoon of lemon zest and the last bit of sugar. Sprinkle the mixture on top of muffins.

Place muffins in the oven, baking for 20-25 minutes, or until they are golden brown on top. Allow muffins to cool remaining in the pan for about 10-12 minutes. Place muffins on a wire rack, allowing to cool another five minutes and then serve warm.

# Vegetable and Egg Breakfast Scramble Recipe

It is important to get plenty of protein for breakfast. This clean eating breakfast recipe packs in great protein with the eggs and the veggies really add freshness and flavor to the scramble. Use the veggies in the recipe or swap them out with some of your favorite vegetables or those you have on hand.

**What You'll Need:**

1 tomato, medium sized, seeded and then chopped finely
1 ½ teaspoon of fresh dill or use a ½ teaspoon of dried dill weed
1 teaspoon of olive oil
½ cup of red onion, chopped finely
4 egg whites
4 eggs
¼ teaspoon of salt
1/8 teaspoon of black pepper, freshly ground
2 tablespoons of water
Nonstick cooking spray

**How to Make It:**

Take a large skillet, coating it with the nonstick spray. Add in the olive oil and begin to warm, then adding the onion and sautéing onion for about 2 minutes. Add in the tomato, continuing to sauté for another couple minutes or until they have become tender. Place tomatoes and onions and a small bowl to the side.

In a large bowl, add the rest of the ingredients and whisk them together. Again, use cooking spray to coat the skillet, then add in the egg mixture. Cook the eggs on medium, stirring on a regular basis until the eggs have almost set. Add in the sautéed tomatoes and onions. Cook a bit longer until the eggs have set completely and are thoroughly heated. Serve hot.

# Walnut and Banana Clean Eating Oatmeal Recipe

Oatmeal is great for your heart, but it may not be fun to eat on its own. This recipe adds plenty of flavor to oatmeal and the addition of bananas adds fruit, flavor and great nutrients. The walnuts add some healthy fats to the mix as well. If you think oatmeal is bland for breakfast, this recipe will definitely change your mind.

**What You'll Need:**

½ banana, sliced
1 tablespoon of pure maple syrup
1 cup of steel cut oats, cooking according to package directions
½ tablespoon of chopped walnuts

**How to Make It:**

Start by cooking the oats using the directions on the package. Drizzled the cooked oats with the maple syrup, mixing to distribute the syrup. Top with the sliced bananas and chopped walnuts. Makes only a single serving.

# Clean Eating Vegetarian Eggs Benedict Recipe

Whether you are not a fan of ham or you just want to go vegetarian, this recipe eliminates ham from eggs benedict, using plenty of great veggies instead. Portobello mushrooms are used instead of ham, adding plenty of wonderful flavor to the breakfast dish. This makes four servings.

**What You'll Need:**

6 cups of baby spinach, packed
¾ cup of sharp cheddar cheese, low fat
3 cups of Portobello mushrooms
2 tablespoons of whole wheat, white flour or you can substitute in almond flour
2 teaspoons of extra virgin olive oil
10 egg whites
1 cup of milk
½ teaspoon of black pepper, freshly ground and divided
¼ teaspoon of sea salt
4 whole grain English muffins, sliced in half and then toasted lightly

**How to Make It:**

Heat a heavy saucepan on medium, placing flour in the pan and slowly adding in milk. Use a whisk to blend together the milk and flour. Allow the mixture to cook until it thickens, which will take 5-8 minutes. Remove the flour mixture from the heat, adding ¼ teaspoon of black pepper, cheese and salt. Stir together until cheese melts.

Use a nonstick skillet to heat up a teaspoon of the olive oil on medium. Add the mushrooms, spinach and the leftover black pepper. Sauté until the mushrooms become tender and the spinach has wilted.

In another skillet, add another teaspoon of the olive oil. Pour egg whites into the skillet, scrambling them for 4-5 minutes. Divide up the egg whites among English muffins, then topping the eggs with the mushrooms and spinach. Top with the cheese sauce, serving up while hot. Makes four servings.

# Clean Eating Homemade Granola Recipe

Once you make this granola, it is easy to store it in your fridge. In fact, you can store it for two weeks, making it easy to reheat this recipe for breakfast on busy mornings. With minimal preparation, you can make a tasty granola that provides a delicious and filling breakfast. Double the recipe to make 16 servings that will last for a big family.

**What You'll Need:**

1 cup of unpeeled apple, shredded coarsely
¼ cup of honey
Milk of choice
¼ cup of water
3 cups of rolled oats
½ cup of toasted wheat germ
1 teaspoon of vanilla
1 ½ teaspoons of ground cinnamon
Fresh berries of choice, i.e. strawberries, blueberries or raspberries

**How to Make It:**

Preheat oven to 325F.

Prepare a baking sheet with some nonstick cooking spray.

In a large bowl, combine together the wheat germ, apple and oats until well mixed. In a medium saucepan, combine the cinnamon, honey and water, allowing to boil. When it reaches a boil, immediately remove the saucepan from the heat. Pour in vanilla, stirring well. Pour the honey mixture over the oat and wheat germ mixture. Toss well until the oats and wheat germ are well coated. Then, spread the mixture out over the prepared baking sheet.

Bake for 45 minutes or until the mixtures turns golden brown. Stir from time to time. Remove from the oven, spreading out the granola on some foil to cool. Mixture should be cooled for at least 30 minutes before you serve it. Eat with milk and fresh berries. Store leftovers in an airtight container.

# Chapter 7: Clean Eating Diet Recipes for Appetizers and Snacks

Goat Cheese Stuffed Cherry Tomatoes Recipe
These appetizers are easy to make, high in calcium and low in fat. The goat cheese adds plenty of great flavor and all the herbs really make this healthy appetizer have a big taste. Serve it up for a snack or serve it at a dinner party for an appetizer that everyone will enjoy.

**What You'll Need:**

25 cherry tomatoes
3 tablespoons of yogurt, low fat
1 teaspoon of freshly chopped rosemary
1 tablespoon of fresh, chopped chives
3 ounces of goat cheese
1 teaspoon of fresh, chopped thyme
1 tablespoon of fresh, chopped dill

**How to Make It:**

In a food processor, combine the yogurt and goat cheese, processing until the mixture becomes creamy.

Place creamy mixture in a medium bowl, mixing in the herbs.

Take cherry tomatoes, cutting them in half and removing the seeds and pulp. To ensure tomatoes stand straight, slice the bottoms of each one. Then, fill each half with about half a teaspoon of the filling. Serve immediately or store leftovers in the refrigerator for two days.

# Clean Eating Potato Skins

Potato skins make a wonderful appetizer, especially for parties that are pretty casual. They are great game day appetizers and wonderful for kids as well. While potato skins are often pretty high in fat and calories, this clean eating version is much better for you and only has four grams of fat per serving. You can enjoy this delicious appetizer without any guilt.

**What You'll Need:**

4 slices of turkey bacon, nitrate free
3 tablespoons of green onions, chopped
1 teaspoon of extra virgin olive oil
1/8 teaspoon of sea salt
1 ½ ounces of cheddar cheese, low fat, shredded
1/8 teaspoon of garlic powder
¼ cup of sour cream, low fat preferred
4 medium baking potatoes
Pinch of paprika
Pinch of cayenne pepper

**How to Make It:**

Preheat the oven to 425F.

Wash potatoes thoroughly, using a fork to pierce several holes in them. Use ¼ teaspoon of olive oil to rub potato skins. Bake for an hour right on the oven rack. Remove from oven and allow to cool for a couple hours.

After potatoes have cooled, preheat oven back to 425F. Slice potatoes lengthwise, removing the centers but leaving about ½ inch of the shell. Use a bit of olive oil to oil a baking sheet, then place the skins on the sheet. Brush with a bit more olive oil, sprinkling with the salt, cayenne pepper, paprika and garlic powder. Bake at 425 for 10 minutes.

Over medium high heat, heat a small pan. Cook bacon until crispy. Drain cooked bacon on a paper towel to eliminate some of the fat.

When potato skins are done, sprinkle them with onion, bacon and cheese. Place back in the oven, baking for another 15 minutes or until the skins have browned lightly. Remove from oven. Top each potato skin with sour cream. Serve while hot. Makes four servings.

# Homemade Clean Eating Guacamole Dip Recipe

Guacamole can be pretty bad for you if you buy a store bought version. Make this recipe to make sure it goes along with your clean eating diet. It is wonderful as a veggie dip, which makes a wonderful appetizer tray when you are having guests over. It is also delicious as a nice addition to any sandwich.

**What You'll Need:**

1 red onion, minced
1 tomato, well ripened
1 tablespoon of lime juice, freshly squeezed
1 cup of cilantro leaves, chopped roughly
2 avocados, ripened
Pepper to taste
Sea salt to taste

**How to Make It:**

Slice tomato in half, squeeze out the juice and seeds. Chunk up the rest of the tomato flesh, setting to the side.

Remove avocado flesh, placing into a bowl. Mash the

flesh up with a fork, allowing some chunks to remain. Then, stir the cilantro, tomato, pepper, lime juice, salt and onion into the avocado.

Serve the dip right away, storing any leftovers in an airtight container in the refrigerator for 2-3 days.

# Pita Pizza Appetizers Recipe

These mini pita pizzas are guilt free and they are a big hit as a snack for the kids or a fun appetizer that every guest will enjoy. Add some ground turkey or chicken if you want to turn these little pizzas into a full meal. It is easy to make, offering fast preparation that allows you to spend more time enjoying your guests when you are having a big party.

**What You'll Need:**

Grapeseed or olive oil
Some kind of natural pizza sauce or try making your own
Mini Pitas, 100% whole wheat
Part skim mozzarella cheese, shredded

**How to Make It:**

Preheat oven to 400F.

On a cookie sheet, arrange the mini pitas, brushing them lightly with a bit of olive oil. Top with the natural pizza sauce, then sprinkle with desired amount of shredded mozzarella cheese. Bake at 400 until the cheese has totally melted and pitas are lightly crisped. Carefully watch pitas, since they cook quickly.

# Tasty Clean Eating Blueberry Muffins Recipe:

If you are looking for a sweet, delicious snack to add as an appetizer for a brunch or just something to enjoy for a sweet snack in the evening, these blueberry muffins are sure to be a hit. They fit in with your clean diet and you will be amazed that they only have 166 calories in each muffin.

**What You'll Need:**

2 tablespoons of butter, unsalted and melted

2/3 cup of sucanat, plus 3 tablespoons, divided

2 cups of almond flour, plus 3 tablespoons, divided

½ teaspoon of salt, plus 1/8 teaspoon

1 ½ teaspoon of cinnamon

2 cups of frozen (thawed) or fresh blueberries

2 teaspoons of baking soda

¼ teaspoon nutmeg, plus 1/8 teaspoon

1 cup of buttermilk, low fat,

2 teaspoons of baking powder

3 tablespoons of applesauce, unsweetened

1 egg

**How to Make It:**

Preheat the oven to 375F.

Prepare a muffin pan with cooking spray or some paper liners.

To prepare the topping, combine the ½ teaspoon of cinnamon, 1/8 teaspoon of salt, 1/8 teaspoon of nutmeg, 3 tablespoons of sucanat, and 3 tablespoons of flour in a bowl. Add in the butter, using a fork to stir until the dry ingredients are moistened. Set to the side.

In a larger bowl, combine the ¼ teaspoon of nutmeg, baking soda, baking powder, ½ teaspoon of salt, 1 teaspoon of cinnamon, 2/3 cup of sucanat and the remaining flour together. Fold blueberries into the mix.

Whisk together applesauce, buttermilk and egg together in a medium-size bowl. Combine with the blueberry mixture, combining until moistened. Avoiding overmixing. Add mix to the muffin cups, dividing up evenly.

Take the topping, crumbling it on top of the muffins. Place in the oven, baking for 18 minutes, rotating the pan when halfway through the baking time. Take muffins out of the oven, allowing to set to cool for about five minutes. Remove the muffins, placing them on a wire rack to cool. Makes 1 dozen muffins.

# Tasty Onion Party Dip Recipe

If you are throwing a party, this clean living onion dip will definitely be a hit served up with fresh veggies. You may want to double the recipe to make sure you have plenty. Garnish with a bit of parsley to make it look great.

## What You'll Need:

1 ½ cup of chopped onions
2 teaspoons of extra virgin olive oil
1 cup of nonfat yogurt, plain

## How to Make It:

On medium high heat, heat up a saucepan. Add in the olive oil, allowing to warm. Then, add the onions to the pan. Stir from time to time. Allow onions to cook for about 10 minutes until they become golden brown.

Remove onions from heat, allowing them to cool thoroughly. Place yogurt and onions in a food processor, processing until completely smooth. Allow to chill for an hour or more before you serve. Serve up the dip with whole grain crackers, vegetables or some pita chips.

Makes 1.5 cups of dip.

## Toasted Pumpkin Seed Recipe

Pumpkin seeds are extremely good for you, since they are full of important nutrients and vitamins that your body needs, such as magnesium. They make a wonderful crunchy snack that is extremely healthy for you. The great part about this recipe is that it is a clean recipe that you can add to your clean eating diet. They are easy to make and do not take long to complete. You might want to double or triple the batch because they are so tasty.

**What You'll Need:**

Small amount of olive oil
Salt to taste
2 tablespoons of pumpkin seeds

**How to Make It**:

Preheat the oven to 250F.

Wash pumpkin seeds thoroughly, then allow them to dry on some paper towels.

Once seeds are dry, prepare a baking sheet with a bit of

olive oil. Spread pumpkin seeds out on the sheet in a single layer. Bake for an hour or longer, ensuring seeds are totally dried. From time to time, shake the pan a bit.

When almost done, increase heat to 350F, baking for another 5-7 minutes, creating lightly browned seeds.

Remove from oven, allowing to cool. Salt to taste. Keep leftovers stored in a closed, airtight container.

# Easy Chocolate Covered Banana Appetizers

Sometimes it is nice to have something sweet as an appetizer. These bananas are made on a stick, so they are easy for guests to handle when you serve them up as an appetizer. Of course, you can always make them for an evening snack when you are craving something sweet as well.

**What You'll Need**

1 tablespoon of coconut oil
1 ounce of pecans, chopped
1 cup of semi-sweet chocolate chips
4 bananas, still a bit firm, peeled
Popsicle sticks

**How to Make It:**

Use wax paper to cover a cookie sheet. Slice bananas crosswise in halves. In each half, carefully insert a popsicle stick, placing the banana on the cookie sheet. Freeze bananas on the sheet for 1 ½ to 2 hours.

Once frozen, melt the coconut oil and chocolate in a medium saucepan. Continuously stir while melting.

Allow chocolate to stand for about a minute after melting, pouring it into a tall glass. Then, dip banana halves in the glass, covering the bananas with the chocolate. Rotate bananas to ensure they are well covered. Roll bananas immediately in the chopped pecans.

Serve right away or put back in the freezer for another hour. Any leftovers should be kept in the freezer in an airtight container.

# Chapter 8: Delectable Dessert Clean Eating Recipes

## Clean Eating Chocolate Chip Cookie Recipe

Just because you are on the clean eating diet does not mean that you have to give up recipes. However, clean eating will require you to look for healthier dessert recipes. This clean eating cookie recipe allows you to enjoy chocolate chip cookies the clean way.

**What You'll Need:**

1 large egg
¼ teaspoon of sea salt
¾ cup of sucanat
½ teaspoon of baking soda
3 ounces of dark chocolate chips, at least 70% cocoa
1 cup of natural peanut butter or almond butter, unsalted

**How to Make It:**

Preheat the oven to 350 F.

Stir together all ingredients except the chocolate, combining well. Then, stir in the chocolate chips. Drop mixture by tablespoonfuls on baking sheets that have been lined with parchment or wax paper.

Bake the cookies for 10-12 minutes. Allow to cool for several minutes on the baking sheet, then placing cookies on a wire rack to finish cooling.

# Chocolate Chip Clean Eating Muffins Recipe

Both adults and kids will enjoy these amazing muffins. Instead of buying muffins that do not fit into your clean cooking regimen, this recipe allows you to enjoy muffins that are made with clean ingredients. Make plenty of them and feel free to freeze them for easy storage.

**What You'll Need:**

½ cup of sucanat
2 teaspoons of baking powder
½ teaspoon of salt
1 cup of applesauce
¼ teaspoon of vanilla extract
½ cup of semisweet chocolate chips
1 teaspoon of vanilla
¾ cup of oat flour
1/3 cup of cocoa powder
½ teaspoon of baking soda
¼ teaspoon of almond extract
Light dash of cinnamon

**How to Make It:**

Preheat the oven to 375F.

Prepare a muffin tin with baking cups or use nonstick cooking spray.

Combine ingredients together in a large bowl. When well combined, add batter to muffin cups, dividing up evening.

Bake muffins for 20 minutes or until a toothpick inserted in a muffin center comes out completely clean.

# Creamy Clean Eating Banana Dessert Recipe

When you want something sweet but healthy, this banana based dessert recipe is a delicious idea. You can choose to garnish it with either dark chocolate or some cinnamon – both taste amazing. This recipe is also easy and quick to make, so you can whip it up in no time when you need something tasty for dessert.

**What You'll Need:**

6 ounces of cottage cheese
2 bananas, cut into ¼ inch slices and divided
1/3 cup of sucanat
6 ounces of cream cheese
1 teaspoon of vanilla
Grated dark chocolate or cinnamon for topping

**How to Make It:**

Use a 9-inch square pan, adding half of the banana slices to the pan and setting to the side. Then, in a mixing bowl, mix together the vanilla, cream cheese, sucanat and cottage cheese until well blended. Spread approximately half of the cheese mixture on the banana slices, then layering in the rest of the banana, topping again with the cheese mixture. Top with chocolate or cinnamon, putting in the fridge to chill for at least an hour before serving.

# Dark Chocolate Clean Eating Cookies

If chocolate is your major craving, these cookies are sure to meet it. It uses dark bittersweet chocolate for a deep, rich chocolate flavor. When you bite into one of these cookies, it will be hard to avoid having another one. Kids love them and they are decadent enough to please the palate of adults as well.

**What You'll Need:**

3 egg whites, from large eggs
1/3 cup of unsweetened cocoa powder
1 ½ cups of sucanat, divided
6 ounces of dark chocolate, chunked
4 ½ teaspoons of arrowroot powder
½ teaspoons of vanilla

**How to Make It:**

Preheat the oven to 375 F.

Use some olive oil to lightly prepare two baking sheets.

In a microwaveable bowl, add chocolate and then microwave for a minute. Remove and stir, then microwaving on high for another minute. Set to the side and allow to cool.

Beat egg whites on high with a mixer, stopping when soft peaks begin to form. Gradually add in a cup of the sucanat, beating it in until the mixture becomes very creamy. Add in the vanilla.

In another bowl, combine the arrowroot powder, cocoa and leftover sucanat. After combined, beat the mixture into the egg white mixture on low. Then, add the warm chocolate to the mix, stirring until you have a thick mixture.

Drop by tablespoonfuls onto the baking sheets, placing in the oven to bake at 375 for 10 minutes. Allow to cook on the baking sheet for 10 minutes, then placing on wire racks to finish cooling.

# Creamy Orange Cranberry Parfait Recipe

The combination of orange and cranberry flavors is delectable in this recipe. It is packed full of healthy ingredients but it still tastes like a delicious dessert. It is especially good during the hot summer months. You will enjoy cooling off with this yummy dessert recipe. Since it only makes one serving, you may want to double or quadruple the recipe so you can make more servings to share.

**What You'll Need**:

1 teaspoon of ground flaxseeds
1 teaspoon of orange zest
1 tablespoon of dried cranberries
1 cup of Greek yogurt, nonfat
½ teaspoon of vanilla
1 tablespoon of chopped walnuts, unsalted
1 orange, peeled and then sliced or sectioned

**How to Make It:**

In a medium bowl, combine together flaxseeds, orange zest, vanilla and yogurt, mixing until well combined. Place half of the mixture into a glass, topping with half of the walnuts, cranberries and orange slices. Add in the rest of the yogurt mixture, then top with remaining walnuts, cranberries and orange slices. You may want to double this, since it only makes a single serving.

# Chapter 9: Easy Clean Diet 5-Day Meal Plan

Whether you are just starting out on the clean eating diet or you just need a bit of extra help, a helpful five day meal plan can help you learn more about how you should be eating. The following is an easy clean diet five-day meal plan you can follow using the recipes provided within this clean eating cookbook.

## Day 1:

Breakfast:
Walnut and Banana Clean Eating Oatmeal

Lunch:
Salsa, Black Bean Mexican Style Pizza

Dinner:
Red Onion Tenderloin Steaks
Crispy New Potatoes with Garlic
Broccoli Spears

Snack:
Toasted Pumpkin Seeds with a piece of fruit

## Day 2:

Breakfast:
Clean Eating Vegetarian Eggs Benedict Recipe

Dinner:
Fruity Salmon Recipe
Side Salad with Veggies
100% whole grain roll

Snack:
Goat Cheese Stuffed Cherry Tomatoes

## Day 3:

Breakfast:
Vegetable and Egg Breakfast Scramble Recipe
1 100% whole wheat English muffin
2-3 sliced strawberries

Lunch:
Premade Vegetable Salmon Kabobs
Served with Brown Rice

Dinner:
Stir Fried Beef Recipe

Snack:
Homemade Clean Eating Guacamole Dip
10 carrot sticks and 10 celery sticks

## Day 4:

Breakfast:
Oatmeal and Apple Pancakes
1 Poached Egg

Lunch:
Chopped Chicken Salad

Dinner:
Delicious BBQ Pork
Fresh Corn on the Cob
Clean Eating Cole Slaw

Snack:
Tasty Clean Eating Blueberry Muffins

## Day 5:

Breakfast:
Mushroom and Sausage Mini Quich
100% whole wheat toast with pure fruit preserves

Lunch:
Leftover Delicious BBQ Pork sandwich with 100% whole wheat bread
Piece of fruit

Dinner:
Stuffed Mediterranean Chicken Breast
Mozzarella Smothered Mushrooms
Honey Glazed Baby Carrots

Snack:
Easy Chocolate Covered Bananas

Made in the USA
San Bernardino, CA
19 April 2013